SCHOLASTIC
News
Nonfiction Readers

Mars

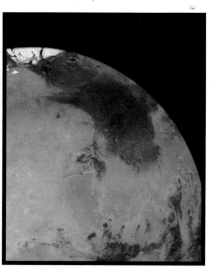

by
Melanie Chrismer

SCHOLASTIC INC.
New York   Toronto   London   Auckland   Sydney
Mexico City   New Delhi   Hong Kong   Buenos Aires

These content vocabulary word builders
are for grades 1-2.

Consultants: Daniel D. Kelson, Ph.D.
Carnegie Observatories
Pasadena, CA
and
Andrew Fraknoi
Astronomy Department, Foothill College

Curriculum Specialist: Linda Bullock

Book Design: Simonsays Design!

ISBN 0-516-25080-9

12 11 10 9 8 7 6 5 4 3   6 7 8 9 10/0

Printed in Mexico.   08

First Scholastic paperback printing, October 2005

CONTENTS

WORD HUNT

Look for these words as you read. They will be in **bold**.

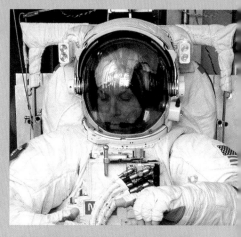

astronaut
(**as**-troh-nawt)

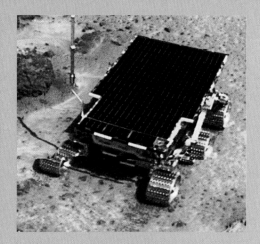

rover
(**roh**-ver)

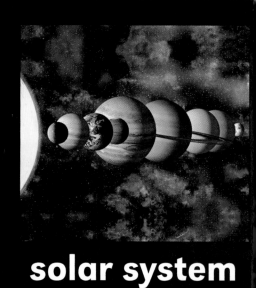

solar system
(**soh**-lur **siss**-tuhm)

4

astronomer
(uh-**stron**-uh-mur)

Mars
(mars)

space suit
(spayss soot)

telescope
(**tel**-uh-skope)

Mars!

There is a shiny object in the night sky that is not a star.

It is the planet **Mars**!

You can see Mars without a **telescope**.

Mars

Stars are not the only shiny objects in the night sky.

Mars is the fourth planet from the Sun.

The planets in our **solar system** travel around the Sun.

Sometimes Mars looks red. It is also called the Red Planet.

Earth

Mars

Mars is next to Earth.

No person has gone to Mars yet.

Only **rovers** have been put on Mars to explore it.

One day **astronauts** may go to Mars.

This rover sets out to explore a rock on Mars.

Astronomers use telescopes to study Mars.

They are studying how people might live there one day.

Mars is close to Earth. We could fly there in a spacecraft.

An astronomer uses a telescope to study the planets.

Mars has a North Pole and a South Pole, just like Earth.

But mostly Mars is different from Earth.

Mars has wild weather, like giant sandstorms.

Mars has two moons.

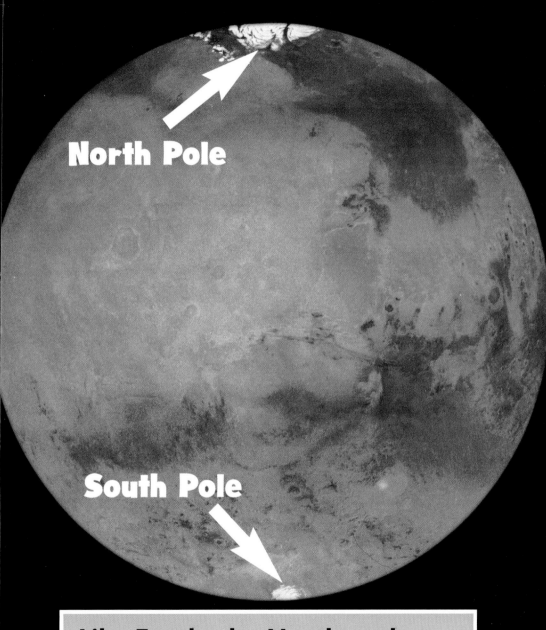

North Pole

South Pole

Like Earth, the North and South Poles on Mars have ice.

Mars is cold all the time.

Humans cannot breathe the air on Mars.

You would have to wear a **space suit** to breathe and stay warm on Mars.

Scientists are looking for signs of life on Mars.

They think people can live on Mars someday.

Do you want to live on Mars?

Is this what a city on Mars might look like?

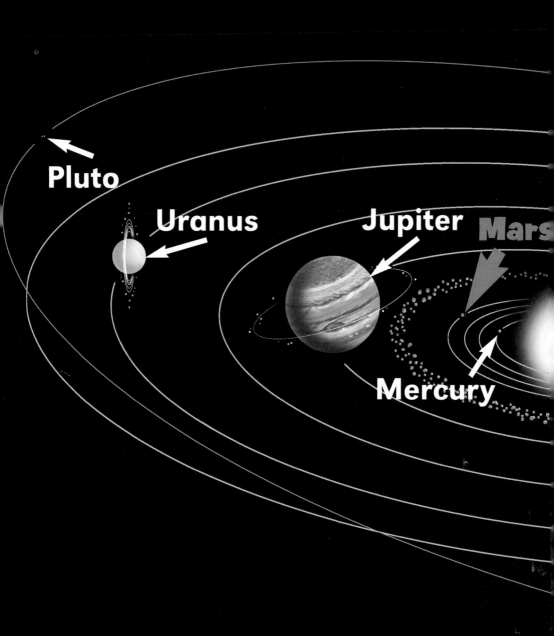

Pluto

Uranus

Jupiter

Mars

Mercury

MARS

IN OUR SOLAR SYSTEM

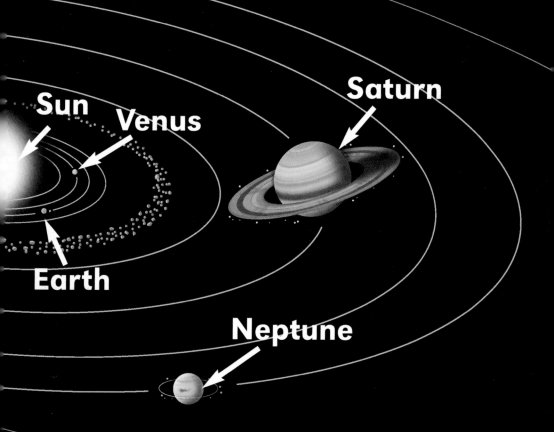

Sun

Venus

Saturn

Earth

Neptune

YOUR NEW WORDS

astronaut (**as**-troh-nawt) a person trained to travel in space

astronomer (uh-**stron**-uh-mur) someone who studies stars, planets, and space

Mars (mars) a planet named after the Roman god of war

rover (**roh**-ver) a robot used to explore space

solar system (**soh**-lur **siss**-tuhm) the group of planets, moons, and other things that travel around the Sun

space suit (spayss soot) special clothing to wear in space

telescope (**tel**-uh-skope) a tool used to see things far away

Earth and Mars

A year is how long it takes a planet to go around the Sun.

 Earth's year
=365 days

 Mars' year
=687 Earth days

A day is how long it takes a planet to turn one time.

 Earth's day
= 24 hours

 Mars' day
= 24-25 Earth hours

A moon is an object that circles a planet.

 Earth has
1 moon

 Mars has
2 moons

Olympus Mons, the biggest volcano on Mars, is 3 times as tall as Mount Everest.

INDEX

FIND OUT MORE

Book:

Mars Darlene R. Stille, Child's World, 2003

Website:

Mars Information and Pictures
http://www.nineplanets.org/mars.html

MEET THE AUTHOR:

Melanie Chrismer grew up near NASA in Houston, Texas. She loves math and science and has written 12 books for children. To write her books, she visited NASA where she floated in the zero-gravity trainer called the Vomit Comet. She says, "it is the best roller coaster ever!"